RaspBerry Pi 3

How to Start

Beginners Guide Book

By William Rowley

Copyright©2017 by William Rowley

Table of Contents

Introduction 5

Chapter 1- Accessories Needed 6

Chapter 2- Installing Windows 10 IOT Core Insider Preview 23

Chapter 3- Installing Raspbian Jessie 25

Python 3 46

Chapter 4- Bluetooth and WiFi Setup 50

Chapter 5- Interfacing the Ultrasonic Sensor with Raspberry Pi 3 62

Chapter 6- RetroPie on the Raspberry Pi 3 72

Conclusion 77

Disclaimer

While all attempts have been made to verify the information provided in this book, the author does assume any responsibility for errors, omissions, or contrary interpretations of the subject matter contained within. The information provided in this book is for educational and entertainment purposes only. The reader is responsible for his or her own actions and the author does not accept any responsibilities for any liabilities or damages, real or perceived, resulting from the use of this information.

The trademarks that are used are without any consent, and the publication of the trademark is without permission or backing by the trademark owner. All trademarks and brands within this book are for clarifying purposes only and are the owned by the owners themselves, not affiliated with this document. **

Introduction

The Raspberry Pi is a commonly used device for programming as well as the playing of games. These devices are commonly used to teach the basics of computer science to kids in schools. They are also a good way for you to teach your kids how to play the common computer games. Raspberry Pi devices have been developed and improved with time, and this has led to the different versions of the Raspberry Pi. The latest version of this is the Raspberry Pi 3, which is the immediate successor of the Raspberry Pi 2. This book is a guide on how to do a number of activities on the Raspberry Pi 3, as well as how to set it up and use it with a number of accessories.

Chapter 1- Accessories Needed

Although the Pi 3 device is small, it comes with ports to which you can attach your peripherals and cables. The device also allows the user to use Wi-Fi and Bluetooth, which are good for improving the user experience. It is made up of 4 USB 2.0 ports as well as an HDMI output, meaning that there is no need for USB hubs for basic use. The device is powered via a micro-USB port, which is similar to the one used on smart phones.

The following are the accessories you may require to use your Raspberry Pi 3 device:

- Suitable Power Adapter.
- Micro SD Card with an SD Adapter.
- A Keyboard unit with mouse or Track Pad
- Display unit compatible with your Pi 3.

Selecting the Power Adapter

A suitable Power Adapter is necessary for you to use your Pi device. On many websites, you are suggested to use a 5 V, 2 Amp Power Adapter. However, the fact is that this is not enough. There is the 5 V 2 Amp, which is usually labeled as "Specially Designed for Raspberry Pi." This cannot be used with the Pi 3, as it is only compatible with the older versions of the Pi. When you power on your Pi3, it has to display a series of rainbow squares, together with a blank white screen. If your adapter fails to do this, then it is not compatible with your Pi 3.

You may choose to use a travel adapter which is widel used with tablets. It has a capacity of 5 volts, 2 Amps and it is compatible with the Pi 3. The problem with this kind of adapter is that will not support the other devices which you will connect to your Pi 3 via the available ports.

The best power Adapter for the Pi 3 device has a capacity of 5.1 volts, 2.5 Amps. From this value, it has an additional 0.1 volt which will serve to compensate for any loss. This Power Adapter looks as shown below:

t has interchangeable heads, you can use it for voltages which range between 100 and 240, and you will see the inside of the adapter. It is a universal adapter which you are free to use anywhere, regardless of the voltage of the power supply, as well as with the different plug points which are used across the world.

This is the best Power Adapter which will allow you to take advantage of your USB ports by using them to plug in other peripherals to your Pi 3 device.

A Wireless Keyboard with a Trackboard

A keyboard is a very important device for data input to the Pi 3 device. You should be aware that your Pi 3 device can accept input from a USB keyboard. Also, know that this keyboard will be drawing power from your Pi 3 device, which under normal circumstances will cause the Pi 3 device to overheat.

The above diagram shows a miniature wireless keyboard having a track-pad which can be used as a mouse. However, the above keyboard has its own source of power, and this will prevent your Pi 3 device from overheating.

The backside of the above keyboard has a battery and a USB Dongle. The USB Dongle can be removed and then installed on any of your Pi 3 USB ports. The keyboard also has a switch for ON-OFF which will help you to switch your keyboard on or off.

The keyboard makes use of a normal Lithium ion battery with 3.7 volts. To charge it, you only have to connect your keyboard to a USB port on a laptop or computer using a micro USB cable, or you may choose to use the normal mobile phone charger so as to charge it.

Touch Screen Display

In this case, you must choose the one which you are able to afford.

The above diagram shows a 7" display which is highly compatible with the Pi 3 device. It has a DSI Ribbon cable, adapter board, and four stands-offs, as well as screws which will help you to make the connections. There are also 4 female-to-female jumper wires for powering the LCD screen as well as the Pi via GPO pins.

When using this display, you will be in a position to create a standalone device which you can use like a custom tablet or mini-desktop computer. The above LCD devices are very compatible with the Raspbian OS, including the latest one (named Raspbian Jessie) as well as with the Windows 10 IOT core for Pi 2. You can also use it with the Windows 10 IOT Core, the Insider Preview for the Pi 3. The touch screen will work very well during the installation process, as well as when you are using the device. Make use of the proper drivers for the touch screen, and you will have a integrated 10 a point touch screen together with an on-screen keyboard, and with this, it will be possible for you to use the Pi 3 device without any external keyboard.

Assembling 7" Touch Screen

This usually comes preassembled with an adapter board which is mounted on the back side of your display, together with four stand-offs as well as the ribbon cables which are needed.

The Display Serial Interface (DSI Ribbon Cable) and the two female-to-female jumper wires form all you need to connect to the display so that you are able to work with your Pi 3 device.

For you to attach your DSI Ribbon cable, follow the steps given below:

- Lift the locking mechanism from the DSI interface on the adapter board, using your fingernail.

- Insert your DSI Ribbon cable into the interface. Make sure that you insert the cable in the correct way. This is shown below:

- Press down on the locking mechanism.

You will then be done.

Assembling the Pi 3 over Touch Screen Display

Note that there are four holes which you can use to attach your Display Adapter Board on your LCD Touch Screen. These are usually aligned the same way as the ones on the Raspberry Pi 3 device. The connection can be done as follows:

- Align your Raspberry Pi 3 over the stand-offs above your Display Adapter.

- Attach your Pi 3 by the use of four screws with stand-offs

Connecting a DSI Ribbon Cable to Pi 3

It is the time for you to attach the Display Serial Interface (DSI) Ribbon Cable from your Display Adapter to the Display Interface of your Pi device. Follow the following steps:

- Lift off the locking mechanism from the display interface on the Pi 3 using your fingernail.

- Insert a DSI Ribbon cable from the Adapter board to the display interface on your Pi 3.

- Press down on the locking mechanism, and then secure the DSI cable

You will be done.

Connecting Power Pins to Jumper Wires

The Pi 3 and 7" LCD Touch Screen may be powered by the use of separate power adapters. Similarly, you can choose to share a single power supply.

In this example, we will be using a 5.1 Volt 2.5 Amp power adapter that can power these two units. The steps given below will help you to share this power supply:

- By the use of the female-to-female Jumper wire, just connect the pin which has been marked as a 5 V on display adapter to the Pin 02 or 04 on your Raspberry Pi .3.

- By the use of another female-to-female Jumper wire, just connect the pin marked as the Ground on the display adapter to the Pin 06 (Ground) on your Raspberry Pi 3.

- You will have then completed the interconnection and sharing of the power supply between the Pi 3 and the Display Adapter.

Connecting the Power Adapter and the Ethernet Cable

There exist 2 Micro USB power connectors which are available on the assembly, one found on the Display Adapter and the other on the Raspberry Pi 3. These are close to each. The power adapter can be connected to any of these. Avoid supplying power to the assembly yet.

The installation of the Operating System requires that the Pi 3 be connected to the Internet. Just connect an Ethernet cable to the Ethernet Adapter of the Pi 3. The other end of your Ethernet Cable should be connected to the LAN Port of a Modem.

You will have completed the assembly of the Raspberry Pi 3 and the 7" Touch screen display.

Selecting a Micro SD Card

The Pi 3 boards do not come with a storage device. An SD card is needed for storage of the operating system. The PI will also be booting from the SD card. The early models of the Pi usually have a slot for the SD card, but the new versions such as the Pi 3 usually support the use of Micro SD cards.

In most of the websites, you are advised to use a Micro SD Card with a storage space of 8 GB. However, this is not enough, and I recommend that you purchase one with a minimum storage capacity of 16 GB. There is not much difference in terms of cost between these two, and this is a good way to ensure that you don't regret your purchase.

SD Adapter for Micro SD Card

You should load or flash the Operating System for your Pi 3 pn some Micro SD Card by use of a Laptop or a Desktop Computer. Card Reader slots which are available in a Laptop / Desktop only supports SD type cards. BY use of an SD adapter, it will be possible for you to read or just write to a Micro SD card connected to a Laptop or Desktop.

Formatting Micro SD Card

The Micro SD Card should be formatted before it can be used. A program named "SD Formatter 4.0 for SD/SDHC/SDXC" can be used. This has to be downloaded and installed on the computer depending on the type of Operating System which is in use. This program can be downloaded from the following link:

https://www.sdcard.org/downloads/formatter_4/

Before starting to format, just insert your Micro SD Card and adapter in the SD card reader slot of your system and then note down the correct drive letter for this from the "My Computer" section. Selecting a wrong drive letter will delete all the data on it permanently, so you must be cautious with this.

Start your SD Formatter program, and then choose the correct Drive letter which is to be formatted. From Options Setting menu, that is, for the Format Type, choose "Full Erase" then Format Size Adjustment "On."Next, click on "OK," and then "Format."

Your SD Card will have been formatted and ready for use.

Download and Extract NOOBS

New Out Of Box Software (NOOBS) refers to the installer for the operating system with the Raspbian OS. It also has a selection for the alternative operating systems such as Windows IOT Core that are downloaded from the Internet and then installed. There exist two versions of the NOOBS, the Offline and the network install version, and then the NOOBS LITE Network install version. One may download a torrent or the Zip file directly from the site This program can be downloaded from the link given below:

https://www.raspberrypi.org/downloads/noobs/

Note that you should download the latest version of the program, and this will provide you with the Raspbian Jesie OS which is supported in the Pi 3 device.

NOOBS is usually downloaded in a WinRAR Zip Archive format. You should have the 7 Zip programs which will help you extract files from this archive.

The 7 Zip program can be downloaded from the page given below, depending on the OS which has been installed on the computer (either 32 bit or the 64 bit for Windows).

http://www.7-zip.org/download.html

You can then extract your WinRAR Zip file into a separate folder. Copy all extracted files to your Micro SD Card that has been formatted. Be careful, as you should copy all the extracted files to your Micro SD card, but not the folder you extracted the files in.

The extracted files will have many operating systems as alternatives. In my case, I copied these to two 16 GB Micro SD Cards. I will use one of these for installing the Raspbian Jessie and the second one for installing the Windows 10 IOT Core Insider Preview.

You can insert the Micro SD card which has the NOOBS and then power up your computer. THE Micro SD card slot for the Raspberry Pi 3 can be found below the Display Serial Adapter on the other side. Insert your Micro SD card that has the NOOBS in this slot, and then plug in the power supply. Your 7"

LCD Touch Screen will display a rainbow square for some seconds and boot into the NOOBS Start-up screen. It is from here that you will be in a position to choose the Operating System you need to use and then install it to your Micro SD Card. The Touch function for the LCD Display works like a charm even before you can install any OS.

Chapter 2- Installing Windows 10 IOT Core Insider Preview

The Pi 3 device has no support for the Windows 10 IOT Core. After you have logged into your Microsoft account, the page for downloading the Windows 10 IOT Core Insider Preview will be opened automatically. It is from this page that you will be in a position to then install this type of OS. Note that the link provided to you only remains valid for 24 hours, after which you will have to request a new link.

The OS comes in two editions, but there is no big difference between these two editions. The next screen will ask you for the edition which you need to download and the device you need to install your OS to. Make sure that you choose the edition which you need to install and the device as the Raspberry Pi. You can then begin the download and install the Windows 10 IOT Core Insider Preview.

Windows 10 IOT Core is not compatible with the Raspberry Pi 3, but the Insider Preview is. The Windows 10 IOT Core Insider Preview usually takes about a minute   to boot. Once the boot process is complete, you will be taken to the Device Info screen in which you will see the name of the device, the type of network, and the IP address as well as the type of OS which is being used.

The tab for Device Settings will allow you to choose the Language and then see the Network & Wi-Fi and the Blue Tooth devices. The Wi-Fi and the Blue tooth devices are yet to be supported. The Power Icon located on the top left allows you to Restart or Shut Down your system. The Windows 10 IOT Core Insider Preview is simply a preview. There is nothing that you are able to do with this OS.

Chapter 3- Installing Raspbian Jessie

It is possible for you to download and then install the Raspbian Jessie OS in your Raspberry Pi 3. Ensure that you download the latest version of the Raspbian Jessie operating system. This one comes in two versions, the first one being the full Desktop version and then the elite version. You can choose to download the torrent or maybe download its zip file directly to your computer.

Note that the file will be downloaded in a zipped format. Once the download is complete, you will have to double click on the downloaded file and you will be allowed to extract it in the folder of your choice.

You may also transfer your image file to a Micro SD Card by use of the Program Win32 Disk Imager which you are able to download for free.

Once your image file has been transferred to your Micro SD Card, just insert it and then power up your Raspberry Pi 3. The Raspbian Jessie OS will take only 25 seconds to boot.

You do not have to type a username or a password. Since this is the latest version of this OS, you will find yourself on the desktop without having to do much.

Installing the OpenCV

The installation of the OpenCV on the Raspberry Pi takes a long time, due to the number of prerequisites which you must first install so as to get started. However, it is good for you to be aware that the installation of this in the Pi 3 is much faster compared to installing it in the Pi 2. Note that in this case, we are installing the OpenCV on a Pi 3 device which is running Raspbian Jessie as the operating system.

Expand the Filesystem

Remember that we have just installed the Raspbian Jessie OS, meaning that the system is brand new. Because of this, we should begin by expanding the filesystem so that all the space within our Micro-SD card can be included. Run the following command:

$ sudo raspi-config

When it prompts you, just choose the first option, which should be "1. Expand File System," and then press the Enter key from your keyboard. Use the down arrow until you are on the "<Finish>" option, and reboot the Pi. The following command can be used to reboot the Pi 3:

$ sudo reboot

Now that once you have rebooted your device, the filesystem should have been expanded so that all the space within your Micro-SD card can be included. To know if this has really happened, you have to run the following command, and then see the result that you get:

$ df -h

Filesystem	Size	Used	Avail	Use%	Mounted on
/dev/root	7.2G	3.3G	3.6G	48%	/
devtmpfs	459M	0	459M	0%	/dev
tmpfs	463M	0	463M	0%	/dev/shm
tmpfs	463M	6.4M	457M	2%	/run

tmpfs	5.0M	4.0K	5.0M	1%	/run/lock
tmpfs	463M	0	463M	0%	/sys/fs/cgroup
/dev/mmcblk0p1	60M	20M	41M	34%	/boot
tmpfs	93M	0	93M	0%	/run/user/1000

The command is "df –h," and gives the result shown above. For demonstration purposes, I am using a card having a total of 8GB and as the above output shows, all of this space has been taken up. However, despite this, 48% of the available space in the card has been used.

The OpenCV together with its dependencies will need some space during the compilation, and it will be good for you to delete files you will not be using and free up your space. If you need to delete the Wolfram engine, just use the command given below:

$ sudo apt-get purge wolfram-engine

This occupies about 700MB of the available space in the Micro-SD Card, and deleting it means that you will have freed this space.

Installing the Dependencies

All the packages which are available should be updated and upgraded first. This can be done by executing the following commands:

$ sudo apt-get update

$ sudo apt-get upgrade

The build process for the OpenCV needs some configuration. This can only be done by use of some developer tools such as the CMake. We should then go ahead and install this tool by use of the following command:

$ sudo apt-get install build-essential cmake pkg-config

The next step should be the installation of image I/O packages which will allow us to load some image file formats from the disk. These file formats include TIFF, JPEG, and PNG. The following command can help us get these:

$ sudo apt-get install libjpeg-dev libtiff5-dev libjasper-dev libpng12-dev

Now that we have installed image I/O packages, some video I/O packages will also be needed. With these packages, we will be in a position to read a number of video files from the disk as well as livestream the various video file formats. The following two commands will allow us to install these:

$ sudo apt-get install libavcodec-dev libavformat-dev libswscale-dev libv4l-dev

$ sudo apt-get install libxvidcore-dev libx264-dev

You don't have to know the purpose for each of the libraries, but know that they will allow us to work with the various video files despite their format.

OpenCV has a library known as "highgui" which we can use so as to build some GUIs, as well as display some images on the screen. For us to be in a position to compile the module, we should begin by installing the GTK Development Library. This can be done by executing the following command:

$ sudo apt-get install libgtk2.0-dev

It is also good for us to optimize the operations which will be done inside the OpenCV. This requires us to install a number of dependencies, and this can be done by executing the command given below:

$ sudo apt-get install libatlas-base-dev gfortran

These dependencies for optimization become very good when you have constrained devices such as the Raspberry Pi. We need to be able to compile our OpenCV together with the Python bindings. This means that we have to install the header files for both the Python 2 and the Python 3. The following command can help us do this:

$ sudo apt-get install python2.7-dev python3-dev

This step should not be skipped, as doing so will result to an error which is related to Python.h, which stands for a Python header file. This error will be shown once you run the "make" command so as to compile the file.

Downloading Source Code for OpenCV

Now that we have installed the necessary dependencies, we can get the archive with the OpenCV from its official repository. The following commands will help us download this archive:

$ cd ~

$ wget -O opencv.zip
https://github.com/Itseez/opencv/archive/3.1.0.zip

$ unzip opencv.zip

Note that in the first command, we began by changing the directory. We then used the "wget" command so as to download the package. The package is downloaded in a zipped format, which means that we have to unzip it. This is what our last command "unzip" helps us to do. A full installation of OpenCV 3 will be needed. The opencv_contrib should also be grabbed. The following command can help with this:

$ wget -O opencv_contrib.zip https://github.com/Itseez/opencv_contrib/archive/3.1.0.zip

$ unzip opencv_contrib.zip

Again, the file will be downloaded in a zipped format, meaning that you will have to unzip it. Also, you might have to use the "<=>" button so as to expand the command when copying and pasting. In some browsers, you may not see the .zip, but don't be worried, as you only have to go ahead and extract your file contents.

It is also good for you to make sure that you download the same versions for both the OpenCV and the opencv_contrib. If you fail to do this, then it will be much more likely that you will get a compile-time error.

The next step should involve the installation of pip, which is a Package Manager for Python. It is also good for us to use the OpenCV together with "virtualenv" and the "virtualenvwrapper."

The virtual environment just refers to a special tool which can be used for keeping the dependencies which are required by the different projects in separate places by the creation of independent, isolated Python environments for each. Execute the following command:

$ sudo pip install virtualenv virtualenvwrapper

$ sudo rm -rf ~/.cache/pip

The command will help you to install both the "virtualenv" and the "virtualenvirwrapper." After that, it will be the time for us to update the file named "~/.profile ~/.profile" so that it can have the lines given below at the bottom:

$ sudo pip install virtualenv virtualenvwrapper

$ sudo rm -rf ~/.cache/pip

Note that for you to add the above lines to the bottom of your code, you will have to first open it in a text editor of choice. Feel free to use the text editor which you are familiar with, and this can be vim, nano, or emacs. You can also choose to make use of the "cat" command and output redirection so as to implement the changes mentioned above:

```
$ echo -e "\n# virtualenv and virtualenvwrapper" >> ~/.profile

$ echo "export WORKON_HOME=$HOME/.virtualenvs" >> ~/.profile

$ echo "source /usr/local/bin/virtualenvwrapper.sh" >> ~/.profile
```

Since the file has been updated, it is good for us to reload it so that the changes we have made can be applied. The reloading of this file can be done by following the steps given below:

1. Logging out and logging in again.

2. Closing the terminal instance and then opening up a new one.

3. Using the source command which is shown below:

$ source ~/.profile

Setting up the Python Environment

We will be using a Python environment for the computer vision development. Let us create this environment:

$ mkvirtualenv cv -p python2

With the above command, we will have created a Python 2.7 environment named "cv." If you need to use the Python 3 rather than the Python 2, you have to execute the following command:

```
$ mkvirtualenv cv -p python3
```

You can then reload your Pi device by logging out and then in again. You should then go ahead to execute the "workon" command so that you can be able to re-access your virtual environment, which is "cv." This command can be used as shown below:

```
$ source ~/.profile

$ workon cv
```

At this point, you should be in your virtual environment, which is "cv." You should be seeing a "cv" which is preceding the prompt. If you fail to see this, then know that you are not in your virtual environment.

Installation of NumPy

If you have been successful so far, you should now be in the virtual environment. NumPy is a Python package which is used for the purpose of numerical processing. This can be installed by executing the following command:

$ pip install numpy

The installation of this package can take some time, so it is good for you to remain patient.

Compiling and Installing the OpenCV

At this point, we should be capable of compiling and installing the OpenCV. Ensure that you are in your virtual environment, and if you are not, you have to run the following command:

$ workon cv

This will take you to your virtual environment. We can then use the Cmake command so that we can setup our build. This is shown below:

$ cd ~/opencv-3.1.0/

$ mkdir build

$ cd build

**$ cmake -D CMAKE_BUILD_TYPE=RELEASE **

```
-D CMAKE_INSTALL_PREFIX=/usr/local \

-D INSTALL_PYTHON_EXAMPLES=ON \

-D
OPENCV_EXTRA_MODULES_PATH=~/opencv_cont
rib-3.1.0/modules \

-D BUILD_EXAMPLES=ON ..
```

Observe the output which you get from the Cmake command. You can then use the "make" command so as to compile the OpenCV. This is shown below:

```
$ make -j4
```

The use of the –j4 option helps us to control the core number to be leveraged during the compilation of the OpenCV 3. There are 4 cores in the Pi 3, and this is why we have supplied a value of 4 so that the compilation can run faster.

Sometimes, when you are using multiple cores, the make may produce errors and this is brought about by race conditions. In such a case, you should begin the compilation by use of a single core. This is shown below:

$ make clean

$ make

In the next step, you should install OpenCV in your Pi 3 device. Execute the following commands:

$ sudo make install

$ sudo ldconfig

The installation of OpenCV should have been done in the "/usr/local/lib/python2.7/site-packages" directory. The "ls" command can help you to verify whether this is the case:

$ ls -l /usr/local/lib/python2.7/site-packages/

total 1852

-rw-r--r-- 1 root staff 1895772 Feb 20 18:00 cv2.so

In some other cases, the installation of this can be done in the "dist-packages" instead of in the "site-packages." Our final step should be to symlink the bindings for OpenCV into our virtual Python environment.

Python 3

After executing the "make install" command, the installation of Python bindings and OpenCV should be done in "/usr/local/lib/python3.4/site-packages." The "ls" command can help you verify whether this happened or not. This is shown below:

$ ls -l /usr/local/lib/python3.4/site-packages/

total 1852

-rw-r--r-- 1 root staff 1895932 Feb 02 22:31 cv2.cpython-34m.so

Note that the created file has been named "cv2.cpython-34m.so," which is not what we want more. We need to have this file named "cv2.so." Let us rename this file:

$ cd /usr/local/lib/python3.4/site-packages/

$ sudo mv cv2.cpython-34m.so cv2.so

Let us the symlink the bindings for OpenCV into the "cv" virtual environment for the Pyton 3. This can be done as shown below:

$ cd ~/.virtualenvs/cv/lib/python3.4/site-packages/

$ ln -s /usr/local/lib/python3.4/site-packages/cv2.so cv2.so

You will then be done.

Testing the Installation

At this point, your Raspberry Pi 3 with Raspbian Jessie operating system has OpenCV 3 already installed. However, before we can begin to do this, it is good for us to test whether the installation of OpenCV was done correctly. You just have to open the terminal, run both the "source" and the "workon" commands, and then try to improve the bindings for both Python and OpenCV. This is shown below:

$ source ~/.profile

$ workon cv

$ python

>>> import cv2

>>> cv2.__version__

'3.1.0'

>>>

The above output clearly shows that the installation of OpenCV 3 was successfully installed in the Python environment.

The OpenCV has been installed successfully, which means that the directories for opencv-3.1.0 and opencv_contrib-3.1.0 can be deleted, and this will help you create a huge free space on your disk. The following command can help you do this:

$ rm -rf opencv-3.1.0 opencv_contrib-3.1.0

However, it is good for you to be cautious before running this command, as you should be sure that the installation of OpenCV was successful before you can delete these. If you make a mistake in this step, then you will experience too many problems during the compile time.

Chapter 4- Bluetooth and WiFi Setup

The Raspbertry Pi 3 has introduced new features, including an amazing WiFi and Bluetooth component. This component can be found along the short edge of your Pi, which is the region in which the micro SD card is inserted. It is a small and white oblong chip antenna which will connect you to the wireless router and enable you to establish a connection to a Bluetooth keyboard or some other device for your Pi.

However, it is good to for you to know that the component is delicate. You have to be careful when installing Raspberry Pi 3 into the case since the position of this chip antenna may result in catching of this. Also, the thick and darker plastic cases may block the signal to and from the chip antenna, which makes the device useless.

Configuring the Wireless Networking

For you to begin using your Raspberry Pi 3, you have to connect it to the router using an Ethernet cable which will help you to get the updates and then configure the Wi-Fi. After booting up of the device, you will be able to plug in the keyboard or establish a connection via VNC or SSH, and then perform the update via the terminal. The update and the upgrade can be done by executing the following two commands:

sudo apt-get update

sudo apt-get upgrade

There are two options on how you can setup the wireless connection. Booting into the GUI might seem to be a bit simple, but doing it from the command line is straight forward.

At this point, you should have a name for your SSID, and if you don't have it, you have to run the command given below:

sudo **iwlist wlano scan**

With the above command, the SSID will be revealed in line "ESSID." In the next step, you can use the following command so as to open the file "wpa_supplicant.conf" in the nano editor. Here is the command:

sudo nano **/etc/wpa_supplicant/wpa_supplicant.conf**

You should then go ahead and edit or add the following:

network={
ssid="SSID"
psk="YOUR WIFI PASSWORD"
}

Hit "CTRL+X" so as to exit as well as save, and then Y and Enter so as to confirm. The wireless connectivity should begin immediately, and if this fails, do the following:

sudo ifdown **wlano**

sudo ifup **wlano**

These commands will help you to restart the wireless device. You first began by putting it down by use of the "ifdown" command and then bring it up by use of the "ifup" command.

If you like to use the Graphical User Interface (GUI), just right click on the Ethernet connection icon which is located on the panel, and then choose the option for wireless networking. The next step should allow you to choose the correct SSID and then add a password. You should be online, and in a position to disconnect your Ethernet cable.

Configuring the Bluetooth

For you to be able to configure the Bluetooth settings on your Pi 3 device, you should begin by updating and upgrading the system by running the commands we used earlier. In the next step, you have to install a Bluetooth package. This can be achieved by executing the command given below:

sudo apt-get install **bluetooth-pi**

You may also choose to install the bluez, which will be installed together with a number of other tools. This can be done by executing the following command:

sudo apt-get install **bluez bluez-firmware**

You will then have installed everything which is needed for the activation of Bluetooth through the command line. To configure Bluetooth for the Pi, run the command given below:

Bluetoothctl

There are a number of options which are provided by this. To see them, you have to type "help" and you will then see them. For Bluetooth to function as you expect, you have to enable it, and make it discoverable so that it may be able to discover the devices. The following three commands can be used for this purpose:

power on

agent on

scan on

The "scan on" command is used for scanning the Bluetooth devices which are around you and which have their Bluetooth enabled. For you to connect to this, you have to enter the connect and then the MAC address.

Connection to Bluetooth Via GUI

This calls for you to install a tool named "blueman." To install this, execute the following command:

sudo apt-get install **blueman**

This will install the tool into your system. For this to be enabled or for you to enable the changes, just restart your device by running the following command:

sudo reboot

The Pi will reboot, and the X desktop will be loaded. You can then click on **Menu > Preferences** > Bluetooth Manager. All the Bluetooth devices which are around you will be listed. To pair, right click on the device and choose connect. Bluetooth will be up and running.

Bluetooth May Fail

Although you may find the process of setting it up straightforward, if your hardware happens not to work correctly, it will not be immediately apparent. It is frustrating for you to run the sudo service Bluetooth status.

How to Connect to a Bluetooth Keyboard

We can easily connect to our Bluetooth keyboard by use of the bluetoothctl command from the command line. The blueman GUI app is not very stable in the Pi 3, and it can easily cause it to crash. The following sequence of steps will then help you to establish a connection to the Bluetooth keyboard:

1. Run the Bluetooth program by executing "bluetoothctl" from the command line.

2. Turn on Bluetooth, if it is not on, simply by typing the "power on" command.

3. Enter the device discovery mode using the "scan on" command if the device has not yet been listed in the devices.

4. Turn on the agent with the "agent on" command.

5. Enter the pair MAC Address so as to do pairing between the devices.

6. You may be asked to provide the pass code on your Bluetooth keyboard. If this happens, just type it on the keyboard, and then press enter.

7. The device should then be added to a list of the trusted devices with a trusted MAC Address.

8. Finally, connect to the device with the connect MAC Address.

If you need to see the list of Bluetooth commands which are supported, you should use the "help" command.

Connecting to a Bluetooth Speaker

Before connecting to the Bluetooth speaker, you should first install the Pulse Audio together with the associated Bluetooth module. The Pulse Audio refers to a sound server which will receive the audio input from the multiple channels and then filter these to a single output or a sink. You can go ahead and then install this by typing the command given below in your command line:

sudo apt-get install pulseaudio pulseaudio-module-bluetooth

Once this has been installed, give Raspberry Pi a quick reboot so as to ensure that everything is in the correct order before we can start:

sudo reboot

At this point, we have everything which is necessary for us to establish a connection to the Bluetooth speaker, and we should go ahead so as to establish the connection. The steps should be as follows:

1. Turn on your Bluetooth speaker and then enter the discovery mode.

2. Open up command line terminal from Raspberry Pi 3, and then run the "bluetoothctl" command.

3. Power on the Bluetooth for the device by executing the "power on" command.

4. Turn on the agent by running the "agent on" command.

5. Scan for the available devices by running the "scan on" command.

6. Pair with the Bluetooth speaker using the pair MAC Address. Note that you should not be prompted to provide any pass code.

7. Add your Bluetooth speaker to list of the trusted devices by use of the "trust MAC Address" command.

9. You can then finally connect to your Bluetooth speaker by running the "connect MAC Address" command.

That is it. Now that the device has been added to the list of the trusted devices, you will be in a position to establish an automatic connection to it once your device is on. You can test your Bluetooth speaker by simply opening YouTube on your browser and playing a video.

Chapter 5- Interfacing the Ultrasonic Sensor with Raspberry Pi 3

We need to use these two and show you how you can read serial data. Note that you should first enable the UART communication on your Pi 3 device. Make sure that you have following equipment:

- Raspberry Pi 3 with operating system

- Ultrasonic sensors with a serial output

- Mini-Grabbers

- Male to female jumpers

- Serial inverter (for ultrasonic sensors which require an inverter)

- DC power supply (for ultrasonic sensors only which will need some separate power supply)

- ESD strap

Enabling the Serial Data

We should now enable the RX pin which is located on the ttyAMA0 so as to receive some asynchronous data. For this to be enabled, the UART setting has to be enabled from the configuration files.

Open the terminal, and then open the "/boot/config.txt" file by typing the following command:

sudo nano /boot/config.txt

The file will be opened on the nano editor. Move to the bottom of your file, and then add the lines of code given below:

enable_uart=1

dtoverlay=pi3-disable-bt

dtoverlay=pi3-miniuart-bt

The lines of code are meant to disable the Bluetooth on your Pi 3 device but instead, serial communication will be enabled. The other versions of the Pi device do not necessarily need this, and their performance will not be affected in any way.

It is time for you to save and then exit the file. You only have to press Ctrl and X at once and then hit the Y so as to save the screen.

Downloading the Python Script

You may find it easy to download or even write your own script. This script will help us to store any data which is collected via the ultrasonic sensor. Consider the simple Pyton script given below:

```
#!/usr/bin/python3
from time import time
from serial import Serial
```

```python
serialDevice = "/dev/ttyAMA0" # default for the
RaspberryPi

maxwait = 3 #

def measure(portName):

    ser = Serial(portName, 9600, 8, 'N', 1, timeout=1)

    timeStart = time()

    valueCount = 0


    while time() < timeStart + maxwait:

        if ser.inWaiting():

            bytesToRead = ser.inWaiting()

            valueCount += 1

            if valueCount < 2:

            testData = ser.read(bytesToRead)

            if not testData.startswith(b'R'):

                continue

            try:

                sensorData        =        testData.decode('utf-
8').lstrip('R')

            except UnicodeDecodeError:

                continue
```

```python
    try:
        mm = int(sensorData)
    except ValueError:

        continue
    ser.close()
    return(mm)


  ser.close()
  raise RuntimeError("Expected serial data not received")

if __name__ == '__main__':
  measurement = measure(serialDevice)
  print("distance =",measurement)
```

The above code is responsible for reading data which comes from Maxbotix ultrasonic rangefinders. The return of the code is the distance to target, and this will be in millimeters. The module can then be used as shown in the following module:

```python
#!/usr/bin/python3


# a script for reading the range values from the
Maxbotix ultrasonic

# rangefinder


from time import sleep

import maxSonarTTY


serialPort = "/dev/ttyAMA0"

maxRange = 5000

sleepTime = 5

minMM = 9999

maxMM = 0


while True:
    mm = maxSonarTTY.measure(serialPort)
    if mm >= maxRange:
        print("no target")
        sleep(sleepTime)
```

```
    continue

if mm < minMM:

  minMM = mm

if mm > maxMM:

  maxMM = mm


print("distance:", mm, "   min:", minMM, "max:", maxMM)

sleep(sleepTime)
```

Power Supply to the Sensor

When you are using the WR ultrasonic sensor and the XL-MaxSonar together with the Raspberry Pi, it is recommended that you should get an external power supply. The intention of the Raspberry is not to supply much power so as to supply such devices.

Connect female end of the jumper to pin 10 of the Raspberry Pi GPIO. This forms the RX pin for the serial data.

Connect a Mini-Grabber or a solder a wire into pin 5 of the sensor, and then connect it to your jumperConnect the sensor to an appropriate power supply.

Installation of the Terminal Software

Minicom is the best software for access to the range data output. Install it by following the instructions given below. Launch your LXTerminal, and then execute the following command so as to install the Minicom:

sudo apt-get install minicom

With the above command, the Minicom software will be installed, and this will help you to read the serial port.

Accessing Range Data Output for Ultrasonic Sensor

Minicom forms the best terminal software for the Raspbian Jessie operating system. The steps given below can help you to access this software and then read the range data:

Launch your LXTerminal, and then execute the following command so as to open the Minicom software:

minicom -b 9600 -o -D /dev/ttyS0

The command will clear the LXTerminal, and you will see a window which appears as shown below:

Welcome to minicom 2.6.1

The number which comes after the ASCII one represents the range reading which the ultrasonic sensor produces. Suppose the reading is R0254, then the range to your target will simply be 254. As your target gets away from the ultrasonic sensor, the range which is reported will also increase. If there exists no target which can be detected, then the maximum range will be reported.

The use of a Raspberry Pi together with an ultrasonic sensor will provide us with an inexpensive way to monitor the tank levels, the height measurement and other countless apps which are in need of the measurement of distance.

Chapter 6- RetroPie on the Raspberry Pi 3

With the RetroPie, it is possible for you to turn your Pi 3 device into a retro-gaming machine. It will build upon EmulationStation, Raspbian, RetroArch, and other projects which will enable you to play your favorite arcade games, classic PC games, and home-console games with minimum setup.

For you to setup this, the following are needed:

- Raspberry PI 3

- MicroSD card

- HDMI cable

- Power supply (5V 2.5A micro USB) or Powerbank

- Ethernet cable to do the initial setup

Installation

The process of installing RetroPie is very easy and smooth. The first step should involve downloading an SD image for the version of Raspberry Pi which you are using. The file comes in a zipped format, so you have to unzip it.

For this to be installed on the SD card, a program known as Wn32DiskManager is needed. This should only apply to Windows users.

Once done, remove the SD card, plug it into your Pi 3, and then power it on. The file system will be expanded automatically, and you will then be taken to the welcome screen from where you will be in a position to configure the controllers.

The Configuration

If you need to perform a configuration on your RetroPie system, you can so by remote connection via SSH. Find the IP from the network, and then use the defaults given below to establish a connection:

- username: pi

- password: raspberry

If you need to see the options which are available, simply run the command given below:

sudo RetroPie-Setup/retropie_setup.sh

A GUI will be presented, and this will have the list of all options which are available.

Xbox One Controllers

Now that you are using SSH, just run the following sequence of commands:

sudo wget https://raw.githubusercontent.com/notro/rpi-source/master/rpi-source -O /usr/bin/rpi-source && sudo chmod +x /usr/bin/rpi-source && /usr/bin/rpi-source -q --tag-update

sudo apt-get install bc

sudo rpi-source

sudo git clone https://github.com/paroj/xpad.git /usr/src/xpad-0.4

sudo apt-get install dkms

sudo dkms install -m xpad -v 0.4

sudo

Once you reboot, just hold any of the buttons on the Xbox one controller. You will see the name of the controller at the bottom. Next, you will see the configuration menu. You can follow the instructions presented on the screen so as to configure the controller.

Note that due to the available regulations, the user must provide the ROMs.

Conclusion

We have come to the end of this guide. The Raspberry Pi 3 forms the immediate successor of the Raspberry Pi 2. Its form factor is similar to that of Pi 2 and Pi 1. The Pi 3 device is compatible with both Pi 2 and Pi 1. The Pi 3 device can be used in schools as well as for general purposes.

www.ingramcontent.com/pod-product-compliance
Lightning Source LLC
LaVergne TN
LVHW052311060326
832902LV00021B/3823